A few thoughts and comments for Throwing Gas on the Fire

"...A fresh metaphor that takes tried and true principles and makes them more accessible to get people in organizations creatively aligned."

David Dame,
Managing Partner,
Key Venture Partners

"...Creates an interesting point for making DRASTIC change. Makes me rethink my methods for customer relationships so they are more interactive..."

Hugh Harrison,
American Red Cross

"...Weaves creativity, insight and wisdom together on how to go about delivering drastic change!"

Austin Reichert,
KeyLink Systems Group

"Creates insights to help you stand out from the crowds and grow your business and then watch for 'drastic' changes in your world."

Patrick Donadio,
MBA, CSP, Master Coach

"... In making the most of your marketing efforts, this little book will trigger your creative side especially for your customer events."

Dr. Glenn Ray,
RayCom Learning

"... If you're ready to make a change, a change for the better, then you have definitely picked up the right book."

Dr. Tom Brett
Brett Family Singers,
Branson, M

Throwing Gas on the Fire

Creating Drastic Change in Sales and Marketing

A business parable for making life **more impressive**, marketing and sales more **profound**, and change more **drastic**.

Written by
Kordell Norton

eScholars

eScholars Publishing
A Division of eScholars LLC
Twinsburg, Ohio

Throwing Gas on the Fire
Creating Drastic Change in Sales and Marketing

By Kordell Norton

Copyright 2007, all rights reserved

First Edition

All characters are fictitious and do not represent any real person. Unattributed quotations are by Kordell Norton.

Cover design: Kym Merrill, Merrill Studios
Page layout: Juan Quirarte, QDesign

ISBN—Soft cover
978-0-9793045-0-7 (ISBN 13)
0-9793045-0-4 (ISBN 10)

Library of Congress Control Number: 2007900756

eSᶜholars

eScholars Publishing
3262 Darien Lane, Twinsburg, Ohio 44087 U.S.A.
Orders@eScholars.net

*Dedicated to Renee, who's
support is unwavering.*

From observing a technology company that used "event marketing", to the commencement address referencing the Greek Sophist's and how they orchestrated and managed change, this book carries the insights of many years. Add the years of testing, utilizing and observation, you have the meat of the material in the story line.

Like the characters in this book, I have used the ideas in the story and can attest to their ability to create great success and impact. They have been used in sales, marketing, management training, adding pizzazz to all types of social events, launching new products, and increasing communication.

The ideas that follow are as old as time. If you feel the concepts are too simple minded, then perhaps you have missed the application of the material. I didn't cover creative thinking or the risks that come with pushing and pulling on the status quo. After reading, if you don't apply the materials, then at least you will have been entertained for a short period.

If you apply the concepts to whatever you are doing, you will find new skills in entertaining and being engaging.

This book is intentionally a short read. Instead of laboring on examples and case studies, I wrote on the premise that a story can teach more than charts, graphs, and carefully notated references.

To those who helped with insights, suggestions, and support, a special thanks to John Roh, Kyle Crisi, Darrell Dalby, Mike Valentino, Doug Smart, and to Jayne Kracker for your editorial insights. Thanks to Jay Scott and Dean Starr for allowing me the creativity to apply the concepts in this book in real life. Most of all, thanks to Renee and my six great kids for their support and love.

Kordell

Kordell Norton
www.KordellNorton.com
(330) 405-1950
Twinsburg, OH 44087

The Present.

The note was typical for him. In his characteristic handwriting it was scrawled . . .

Meet me in the dungeon at 2:00 for a conversation about The Conversation.

Chapter One

The Dungeon... three hours later.

Our office complex consisted of two buildings—one, a tall glass creature where most of the executive offices were located; the second a short concrete job with limited windows and reinforced walls to protect the computer systems from the enemy, be that terrorists or acts of God in the form of foul weather. On its lower floor and a back corner was a conference room, affectionately called the Dungeon. The dark, windowless hall that led to it probably inspired the unique name. It was the ideal location for getting some serious work done without intrusions.

I arrived a few minutes early, dropped my planner on the table and was settling into a chair when he pushed open the door. Brock McCarthy seemed to be cheery to a fault and this afternoon was no exception as he flashed his charismatic smile.

"Hey, Big Guy, how are you doing?" Not waiting for an answer, Brock moved into the room. "I thought we could meet here so we could visit a few minutes without interruptions. I thought you might want to know how I've been doing *it* for the last year."

"Doing what?" I asked.

"How I've been kicking your behind in sales," he said with a wry smile.

"What?" I wasn't quite sure where he was going with this.

"Would you like to know how I am doing it?" he asked.

Actually, I did want to know, even if I wasn't ready to admit it. Although we had both worked for the same company for many years, lately his efforts had become almost legendary. It seemed his team had moved into a different realm. His productivity numbers increased three-fold over where he was in the past. Even working with programs he'd previously introduced, his success seemed to be gaining momentum.

He rested his elbow on the table and cupped his chin in his hand, tilting his head to the side. "I wish I could take credit for what has been happening. The truth is that my success of late is the result of my dad."

He tightened his lips and his eyes moved to the tabletop. I knew about his father's demise, but that was several years ago. Brock McCarthy loved his dad. Although I had never met his father, I felt I knew him in a very personal way, especially since in pictures they looked so much alike—both with a full head of gray hair, square jaw and straight Romanesque nose. Plus, there were the stories of them doing things together. After every family event, Brock had stories to tell. His father had the ability of taking an average activity and turning it into a something to write a book about.

There was the "bubble" experience— a weekend family get-together at the park that turned a picnic into a soap bubble extravaganza. In addition to the food and laughter, there was a small wading pool filled with 10 gallons of a Mr. Bubble type solution and a hula-hoop for giant bubbles. Of course, there was the standard issue bottle of soap bubbles for each of the kids and bubble guns. I would have thought I was doing well to buy my kids a bottle of bubble solution. The McCarthy family, on the other hand, just naturally went beyond the mark.

"Are you telling me that your success is some sort of tribute that you are orchestrating for your father?"

"No. I'm telling you that the success is a result of something my father left for me," he said as he leaned back and focused on me through slightly narrowing eyes, the wry grin slowly returning.

"I don't get it. Your father passed away three or four years ago, but your success has really skyrocketed in just the past six to twelve months. What happened?"

Pushing back from the table, he laced his hands behind his head. "At the time of Dad's passing, I was pretty devastated. Those sad grieving days were filled with going through his stuff and deciding what to keep and what to give away. Because of the funeral and all the arrangements, there were some boxes I just put in my attic figuring I would go through them later. So a little over a year ago, I finally got around to that task. It was in the very last box that I found this."

He set a faded brown leather journal onto the table and gently slid the book toward me. I reached over and picked up the book, the worn leather cover soft to the touch. The journal was about the size of a very thick paperback. I looked up at him and without a word he nodded his permission to open it. Wrapped around the book was a long leather throng that held the book closed. Unwinding the strap, I started to leaf through the pages. I could see a strong hand and various black and blue inks, with journal entries dated over many years. The cursive letters were almost art. Beautiful loops and slants made by someone who developed his handwriting in the days before the typewriter and personal computer.

Brock said, "Its funny how 'time' makes us appreciate history more. That little book is different from the journals that my dad kept later in his life."

He went on. "It was there that I finally found *it*. Dad had said all his life that one of the most significant things that ever happened to him was *The Conversation*. He said that one day he would share it with us, but, you know how busy life can be."

He gestured for me to hand him back the book.

I slid it back across the table and he picked it up and started turning to find an exact page. "Dad would often say that a major portion of his success in life, with his job, his kids and his other interests, were all a result of *The Conversation*. With his death, I thought I would never hear the details, but guess what I found?" He turned the open book to face me, and continued, "The drastic successes for me and my team I can directly attribute to having read *The Conversation* a year ago. Are you a little curious?"

"Are you kidding? I had figured all of your success had come from some business school concept or "how to" book. But it was really... this?"

Brock smiled knowingly. "We don't have much time. I have to get to a meeting, but if you have about fifteen minutes to spare, let me share part of *The Conversation* entry with you."

"Go for it," I replied as I leaned back in my chair.

Brock settled the book in front of him on the table and in his distinctive voice started to read his father's journal.

Chapter Two

... The Journal ...

Spring, 1966—an airport in the MidWest

It was a great conversation.

Applying what I got out of our discussion has brought huge changes in just the short time I have been using it. I don't see this being a short-term thing either. I suspect that I can use the principles I learned in that conversation for the rest of my life.

It had been quite a business trip.
I remember looking out the high windows of the airport terminal, watching the approaching line of thunderstorms. The early spring heat had built these clouds into airplane grounding monsters. I had just finished watching one business traveler have a heated argument with a ticket agent, and had opened a notebook to jot down some things that I needed to do, when the man seated next to me very casually started a conversation. He had that look of a benevolent grand-father in his mid-50s with slightly graying hair, a kind face with a square jaw line and a salt and pepper moustache.

He said something like. . . "It's amazing how, when life comes at us, we react and make choices that bring us so much pain or so much happiness."

His was a low key comment, made while he too watched the final moments of the heated dialog between the traveler and the agent. While we were facing the same direction, I knew the comment was made for my benefit.

I looked over at him, but he didn't immediately turn his head. He told me that his hobby was studying what brought about change in people. Turning and looking me straight in the eye he said he had come to understand that there were common "elements" that could be orchestrated and managed to bring about drastic change. That if we used these elements to our advantage, we could improve and control much of our lives.

This was someone who was thinking a little deeper about life than I currently was. My curiosity was piqued.

He used the example of our current airline as he started to share his ideas on what I have come to refer to as a recipe for drastic change. He pointed out that the airline had a great opportunity to give us a bad or a great experience in the next several hours. He hinted that by not under-standing the elements of drastic change, the airline had done nothing, and now our fellow travelers were steaming over the flight delay.

I asked him if he had defined those elements.

"Well yes," he said. "We all go through change. All the time. Every day brings a whole new set of challenges and experiences. For the most part, the human race does not change that much as life comes at us. We do adapt to our environment, be that Nomads in the desert or Eskimos in the Arctic. But, do we really change that much, day to day?"

For me, this was an especially painful question, as I was struggling to lose a few extra pounds and found it was harder to do than I thought.

Sometimes, he explained, orchestrated experiences occur that bring about massive change in people. Often, these changes are anticipated and looked forward to. In fact, we pay a lot of money to get them. Most of the time we have to pay to have drastic change and this is one of the first elements. There are admissions or dues.

When I asked him what he did for a living he gave a guarded answer. Basically, he said that he tries giving one of life's most positive and enjoyable experiences to people. He said that he was about to undertake a monstrous undertaking that was based on his observation that people will pay handsomely to have a wonderful experience. He thought that his new business venture would create a customer experience that should set a new standard for fun and enjoyment. At the core of his efforts were his elements of drastic change.

I told him that I was hooked and wondered if he would share the elements with me. Now my notepad and pen were at full attention.

He shared with me that there were hundreds of them, but he had narrowed the most influential to just a handful of key elements.

He warned that when I heard them I would probably simplify them in my mind and underestimate their

cumulative effect, indicating that
that would be a great disservice
to the humble student of change.
Examples of their continuous use, he
further noted, were abundant
throughout history.

Glancing at my note taking, he pulled
a yellow pad of paper from his brief-
case. He told me that he could save
me some time as he had just organized
some of the key elements into an
acronym.

Although some of his defining words
were a stretch, I have thought since
then how simple and clear they were
for describing the elements of rapid
change.

Written on the page were:

Dollars

Raiment

Authority

Sounds

Thirst

Illuminate

Calories

He pointed out that he built these elements around the ability to spell the word DRASTIC and that he figured it would help him educate his company's executives easier. He then went on to tell me some ways that he had seen them applied by saying . . .

Chapter Three

Back in the the Dungeon meeting room...

Just then Brock's cell phone rang. Glancing at the caller ID, he flipped open the phone for a brief conversation which culminated with "I'll be right there."

I knew something was up as he closed the phone and turned toward me.

"Hey, Big Guy. Looks like I have a major forest fire on my hands. I really need to go take care of something. Before I scoot, I have a question for you. What do you think about *The Conversation*?"

"My first response is exactly what the guy in the airport said, 'It seems pretty simple.'"

"That was my take too, when I first read the entry. But if you read on . . . well, that is the secret to the huge improvements in my job and my life in the last year.

"I'll tell you what. I think I can share the rest of what is in the journal in the coming weeks. I think you have enough background that we can have some common vocabulary as you see how **DRASTIC** can be applied. Sound OK?"

"Well, do I have a choice?" I said in my best John Wayne impersonation.

With a laugh he said, "Not really," and left the room.

Chapter Four

Three weeks later . . .

Weeks had past since we were in the Dungeon. Life had been so busy that our first chance to talk was at the outdoor wedding of our boss's daughter. The best man and one of the bridesmaids walked past us, arm in arm, laughing at some private joke.

"Can you believe this?" said Brock wide-eyed and with a wave of his arm.

"You could significantly reduce the national debt were the monies spent on this extravaganza given to the Federal Government," I joked with him.

"You couldn't ask for a better example of **DRASTIC** than this," said Brock.

I raised an eyebrow. "Meaning what?"

"Just look at the planning that has gone into this affair so that in one solitary moment, drastic change could occur."

I must have had a perplexed look because Brock jumped right in with his explanation.

"Need I play back the scene of one hour ago? There stood the bride and groom, holding hands as the question was asked, 'Do you agree to be totally different today and from here on out than you were yesterday?' Of course, the question wasn't asked that way. It was more discretely worded as, 'Do you take this man to be your lawfully wedded husband?' But the question could have been worded into its true meaning of, 'Do you agree to end your life as a single person, and to change your lifestyle, thinking, behavior, spending habits, living arrangements, and financial standing for the rest of your life, so help you God?'

"Yesterday they acted as two single adults, with a common interest, and today they agreed to a new and drastically different direction. Is there any more dramatic example of drastic change in this world than that of a newly formed marriage?"

I shrugged, still not quite sure where he was going. "I guess I hadn't thought of it that way. But what about the 'elements' that we talked about a few weeks ago?"

"Ah, well, let's look at it," he replied, looking pleased that I'd remembered the precise terminology.

"If you remember the acronym, **'D'** stood for *dollars*. Look around you and you can start counting the dollars. I could get you another slice of that mouth watering, skyscraper cake. Or take the hundreds of floating flower arrangements on the pool and in the pond over there. The money spent, unbelievable. I guess if you've got it, flaunt it. In my observations, there are times when you don't have to spend dollars to have this drastic change. But the **'D'** really is about the cost of production. Either you or I, or some rich producer, parent or bank is funding the change. Call them what you may, admittance fees, or the price of some service or product, but there is a dollar investment that most often occurs.

I watched as more people moved onto the dance floor, but I was more interested in my conversation with Brock. "So what about the letter **'R'**? I asked.

He grinned. "Well, the **'R'** is kind of a stretch. I think the word my Dad and his new friend at the airport those many decades back struggled with was *raiment*. Not a word we use often these days, but the more modern word 'clothes' plays a big part here. During most times of **DRASTIC** change, there is usually special clothing involved. That wedding gown," said Brock pointing to the bride now dancing with a fun-loving seven-year-old relative of some sort, "represents one of the finest examples of clothes that are planned out, purchased and worn in a **DRASTIC** change event.

Let's also not forget the bridesmaid's dresses, which allow them to participate with their own *raiment* in this **DRASTIC** event. The gowns and tuxedos represent the sort of clothing that occurs during special moments of change. And that's not counting the evening wear of all the friends and relatives, some of which seem to have a faint smell of mothballs, and I am not sure if it is the clothes or the relatives."

Brock and I both reported to the same person at work so our conversation was halted as "the boss" approached. She was in her own conversation with the tall gentleman who had performed the ceremony. Looking up, she saw the two of us and stopped to introduce us to her pastor.

"Gentlemen. I would like you to meet the man who has been the Pastor and sole religious influence in our family for almost 30 years."

After the requisite handshakes, and introductions, the two of them headed off toward the house.

"Let's see if I remember," I said, "the '**A**' is for *Authority*, right?"

"Right," Brock nodded.

"I like what my father took to calling this person in his journal. His exact words were *"A Wizard of the Greatest Magnitude"*. The journal goes on to indicate that *Wizards* carry huge amounts of power and authority. In fact, in the ceremony, he proclaimed his power without beating around the bush. 'By the power vested in me by this great state, I now pronounce you husband and wife. You may now kiss the bride.' Who gave him his power? The State. Who gave the State their power? We, the voters. If we don't like how they use the power we give them, we vote these politicians out of office.

"It seems that the single most common element in almost every incident of **DRASTIC** change is the *Authority* figure, or the *Wizard*. Their titles are diverse, from elected official to boss, from parent to spouse, from captain of the ship to Captain of your soul."

My mind was starting to wander on *Wizard* and momentarily thought of the Wizard of Oz, when a family member of the groom, who had apparently enjoyed his "liquid refreshment" a little too much, tried to get the microphone from the band. We all watched as the groom went about coaxing the microphone from the hapless Karaoke champ.

Brock unbuttoned his shirt's top button and loosened his tie and swatted at a mosquito that was circling his head just before a cool breeze whiffed it away.

"The **'S'** in **DRASTIC** is for *sound*. Had that Karaoke champ really regaled us with his musical talents, we might have something even more entertaining to share back at the office. That aside, the place for *sound* in **DRASTIC** change is one of the most elegant elements. Most of the time, it is music that we associate with the experience. The music of our teen years sticks with us through the rest of our life, reminding us of those years of change. And who can forget that special love song that belongs to our most loving relationships."

I was soaking in all of his words when we were interrupted. "Excuse me, gentlemen," said a man with a silver tray. "Can I get you something from the bar?"

"Nothing for me," I replied.

Brock, however, asked if one of the glasses of Champagne on his tray was available.

"Absolutely, sir," the flummoxed waiter said as he stooped to allow Brock to pluck the crystalline glass off the tray.

Brock took a sip of the pinkish liquid, held up the glass and said, "Ah the **'T'** in our equation. To *'thirst'* then," he announced as he hoisted his glass to an imaginary toast. "It seems that liquid plays a pretty big part in a majority of experiences where change occurs. At a training event, it's the break for soft drinks. For a graduation, it's the beer parties. For a religious event, it's the water of Baptism as a person is proclaimed a 'new creature' and starts a new life."

"Amazing," I said. "I've never thought about how this stuff is orchestrated. Let's see. **'T'** is for *thirst* or *liquids*. And for the letter **'I'**...?"

"The **'I'** is for *illumination* or light. The lights of this evening's party are a perfect example," he explained, gesturing toward them. "There are also the lights of a stage play. Being 'in the spotlight' is the thing in the world today, and especially the lights of multi-media. It seems that electrons are at the core of everything we do now. This is especially true for the younger generation. In fact, those that went through their formative years during the birth of the Internet just expect lights, lumens, and electrons. Those vying for the attention of today's consumer need to realize that their competition is Steven Spielberg or the creators of the latest video game."

I looked out at the sparkling lights shimmering off the swimming pool a few yards away, and the lights of the dance floor with couples locked in embrace to a slow moving love song that dated back a decade or two. With a grin I said, "Well that sheds some light on the subject."

"Yeah," said Brock rolling his eyes. "Remind me to tell you about my friend who called in the president of one of his divisions whose performance was not going well. He told this president to bring his books and expect to talk about the financial numbers under the light of a 'full noon sun.' We 'turn out the lights' on a business or 'shine some light' on a situation.

"And while we are on the subject, you CAN have your cake and eat it too."

"What?" I couldn't keep up. Brock was on a roll now, jumping from subject to subject like a flea in circus.

"*Calories.* It's the last letter . . . **'C'**," he said as he made a hook in the air.

"For us here tonight, the 'C' is easy because the cake is such a traditional part of this event. People love to eat, especially at celebrations. Celebrations and ceremonies are often at the heart of the most pleasant **DRASTIC** changes. If you are putting together a life changing event or memorable experience, you tend to orchestrate food into it somehow."

"Wait a minute," I interrupted, wanting to catch him on an important point before I forgot. "You said 'pleasant drastic change' a second ago. What do you mean 'pleasant'? You think **DRASTIC** could also be used for unpleasant things as well?"

He was nodding his head now. "Even the bad stuff has many of the elements of **DRASTIC** things in them. Earlier today, I had to fire someone at work. ***Dollars*** were involved in a severance package for my unfortunate former employee. ***Authority*** was involved because I had the power to terminate him. Now he will need to decide if he wants to find a new authority figure, a new job. I thought of that as he left and I turned off the lights, the illumination, in his office, how ironic these elements are. In his case, being fired is one of life's most drastic change events."

"Hey guys," said our boss from behind me.

I turned as she sat down in an empty chair at our table.

With a sigh, she reached behind her neck and checked her hair. "Great wedding! At least it better be for all the planning we did. I just wish I had paid more attention to my shoes. They are gorgeous, but pure torture chambers on my feet. So what do you think? Are we sending my sweet daughter off to her new life with a great celebration?"

I grinned and looked at Brock who winked and reached for his glass. I knew our conversation and the late hour would have us finishing this discussion later. As he turned to engage in conversation with the boss, I sat back and breathed in the gathering coolness of the evening and let the lights, smells and sounds of change wash over my enlightened mind.

Chapter Five

Three months later . . .

The conversation at the wedding was weeks behind us now as the summer vacation season arrived, August followed and we moved into fall. Brock and I traveled with new work demands. There were a couple of e-mails from Brock with some kudos on some sales wins my team had, but we literally did not talk for weeks.

"Hey stranger," Brock said. "I don't know who has been busier, you or me!"

My head was down as I checked some last minute figures while walking towards my next meeting. Looking up, I saw him with travel case in tow.

"Uh. . . Good morning" I replied instinctively. "Tell me about it. Are you arriving or are you headed somewhere?"

"Well, the irony is that I am headed for that little Midwest airport where my father had that fateful conversation all those years ago. I am going on a quick overnight trip. Are you around tomorrow? Can we catch up?"

"Tomorrow? Let me see. I think I am here all day," I replied. "I have a meeting with my team until just before lunch; maybe we could catch some lunch."

"That would be great," Brock said as he turned to see the elevator doors slide open several steps away. He walked into the subdued lighting of the elevator, turned, and called back to me as the doors closed. "I will be interested to see what you have done with **DRASTIC**."

Chapter Six

The next day . . .

When I noticed Brock hovering outside my office, I gave him a nod of acknowledgement, and wondered what he'd meant when he said, "to see what I had done with **DRASTIC?**" I had given it some thought, but I don't think that I had seriously done anything with the information since talking about it at the wedding. My team was putting the final touches on sales and marketing for one of our products at the conference table in my office. I gave some last minute assignments and the team filed out. I walked over to my desk, put down my notebook and heard his voice behind me.

"You really don't get it, do you? You haven't done anything with **DRASTIC**, have you?" questioned Brock. He swung the door shut behind him and moved to one of the chairs at the head of the conference table. He laid a letter sized sheet of paper he was holding on the table.

I was clueless. "Huh? What are you talking about?"

"This stuff is like throwing gas on the fire. It takes whatever you are doing and adds pizzazz and life to it. For example."

Turning to the whiteboard, he picked up a marker and in bold letters wrote the word—*Equity*.

"With the speed of change in today's world, people think in terms of brands. A brand allows you to communicate your value and connect with the customer very quickly with imagery. Long the tool of large corporations, the speed of business now is forcing everyone to learn what a brand is and how to create and nurture one.

66 This stuff is like throwing gas on the fire. It takes whatever you are doing and adds pizzazz and life to it. **99**

"Because information is proliferating so quickly, people will take a block of information and give it a name. That way, they can communicate to each other and in their own mind, a bunch of information with a phrase, or in some cases a single word. Often these names and words represent a brand."

He had my full attention, and I focused on his every word. That was a good thing because he clearly had no intention of slowing down.

"For example, someone might label a fellow worker a computer geek. At one point a geek was a kind of circus entertainer. Today, however, a computer *geek* is descriptive and allows us to describe others without getting specific on actual characteristics. But for us, the word geek represents something. It has a place in our mind. We have a mental image of a person. Like the word 'geek,' these mental images of people, places, things, events, and experiences allow us to make sense of the world. Our thoughts and opinions and the actual words we assign to each are valuable. They have real meaning and worth. That's why I choose to call them an *Equity*." As Brock finished, he turned and underlined the word *Equity*.

"I hate to tell you, but I think your definition of the word *Equity* is off a little. I think it has to do with law, property, stocks and bonds or even real estate." I was pretty sure I was accurate in what I was saying.

"Right you are," he said, stabbing the air between the two of us with a pointed finger. "In both cases it represents something of high value. And in the case of a stock or bond, it is a value that can be bought, sold, or traded. In real estate you can get a loan against your equity. It is for that reason I use this word specifically.

"Let's say we take the word "geek" and replace it with a name of a branded product." He again swiveled toward the whiteboard and started writing some popular brand names.

Nike

Coke

Intel

Levi

He turned and pointed to the word 'Levi' and said, "What does this word mean to you?"

"Denim blue jeans."

"Right you are. But to the first customers of Mr. Levi Strauss, it wasn't necessarily the cloth of the pants. You know the story?"

"Oh yes. This one I am familiar with. The California gold seekers of 1849 needed really sturdy pants to deal with the rigors of mining. Levi Strauss found that if he used a heavy canvas-like material he could make pants that would hold up."

"Well, that is part of it" Brock said. "The miners would put their ore samples in their pockets (I mean, who wants to put a piece of gold down on the ground!)

and the weight of their bounty would rip the pockets off the pants. So, our Mr. Strauss figured out that if he put the pants together with rivets, instead of stitching, the seams would never rip and pockets would never give up their treasure. Guess how many rivets he used?"

"There were a certain number?" I asked, scratching my head.

"Sure. Ever heard of 501 jeans?"

A light went on inside my brain.

"Of course, today they don't use 501 rivets. But in the minds of the original Forty-Niners, the brand of Levi represented rivets and strong pockets. The key phrase being *'in the mind.'*

"Today, no one even considers rivets in their jeans. But the value placed on 'Levis' in the mind of the miner allowed Mr. Strauss to build a pretty good business. And businesses and their products can be bought and sold, JUST LIKE EQUITIES.

So now we have products, services, and even companies with names and value. Why?"

"Because in the mind of the customer they have value," I said.

"That is correct. The central point is their value *to* the customer—the person with the dollars to spend!

"So, we have a traditional name we give to this thing the customer values." He turned and put an equal sign to the right of the word *Equity* and then wrote out the word *'BRAND'*.

"A brand is an equity, or value, in the mind of the customer, but more important is what that brand *does* in the mind of the customer."

I had understood everything he had been saying up to this point. "Does?" I asked.

"Think of it this way," he explained. "In the mind of the customer, they spend their money based on what they hope

❝ A brand is an equity, or value, in the mind of the customer... ❞

those purchases will do for them. If they have a successful experience with a particular purchase, they trust that experience and hope they can have it again." He now wrote the word *Experience* under the *Equity = Brand* heading.

"Based on the customers' experiences, an expectation is created," Brock explained as he added the word *Expectation* below and to the right on the whiteboard.

"So the process of building a *Brand* or *Equity* is in providing experiences and expectations and the interplay of these two factors."

I held up my hand. "Wait. What do you mean *the interplay*?" I didn't want to lose him before he continued.

Smiling, Brock replied, "Let me give you an example. When you take the kids to the county fair, do they have carnival rides there?"

"Yes. And all the cheesy ring toss games, the 'guess your weight within a hundred pounds' booths."

Nodding he said, "But what would you be expecting if you went to a Florida theme park?"

"The credit card charges that go with a major event," I replied.

"Right you are!" he said stabbing the air with the marker in his hand. As he spoke he turned and wrote the word *event* down to the left and across with the word *expectation*, so the board looked like:

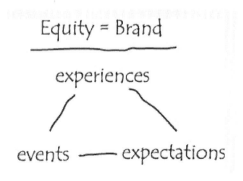

"It is these events, experiences, and expectations that make up so much of the fabric of life. Look at how simple and beautiful the triangle is. Experiences create expectations. Events lead to experiences and then expectations. Sometimes we expect experiences that are the same, and now and then we expect new experiences. Why go back to the same theme park? Because we are expecting some new experiences that measure up to the events of that theme park in the past."

It was then that he noticed my smirk. "What are you smiling at?" he questioned.

"I was just thinking of how dynamic the three factors are. Some customer purchases are made solely on prior expectations. We bought the work of a particular artist because of their previous body of work. If they created great stuff before, then their new stuff should be good. It works for events as well. A professional sporting event probably qualifies. It may or may not be a great contest, but we pay the money and go hoping for a great experience, even if our expectations are sometimes dashed."

"Right you are," he said, pleased that I was catching on. "The very disturbing thing is that our lives are filled with brands. Some of them are official, some not."

"Wait a minute," I interjected as I heard a new term. "What do you mean by unofficial brands?" "Think about your experience with a lawyer, real estate agent, insurance agent, hair dresser or even the family doctor. Even my auto mechanic in his greasy, cluttered space represents a brand in my mind. I wouldn't trust my car to anyone else. All of them represent an expectation, and/or an experience. But do they have deliberate branding with logos, advertising, and a marketing department? Maybe . . . Maybe not."

"Each of us as an individual person represents a ***brand***, he said hooking the air in the classic quote gesture, "whether we are aware of it or not. Our employers pay us according to the experience and expertise we bring to work."

"Keep going," I said, eager to hear more.

"Why all the razzle-dazzle over these 4 'E's' of equity, experiences, expectations and events?" Brock asked. "The reason is that **DRASTIC** is at the core of all of them. It is by using **DRASTIC** that we can speed up, improve, and make the 4 E's more memorable.

"I brought this for you," he said, poking the paper that was lying on the table. "I literally peeled it off the wall of my office."

Sliding into one of the nearby chairs, I gave him a curious look as I took the paper from him. There on the paper was the word **DRASTIC** written vertically down the left side of the page. To the right of each of the letters the defining words that each letter represented. To the right of these defining words were handwritten notes.

"Since our conversation so many months ago, I had a similar conversation with my team members," Brock said. "You will note some of the other words that my team gave as clarifications on our **DRASTIC** words."

Looking down, I scanned the words his
employees had written.

D DOLLARS—ADMISSION FEES, TUITION, BUDGETS,
PARKING, MEMBERSHIP DUES, THE PRICE OF
SOUVENIRS, THE COST OF PURCHASING THE
ITEMS BELOW.

R RAIMENT—UNIFORMS, DRESS-FOR-THE-OCCASION,
GOLF SHIRTS, TRINKETS, HATS

A AUTHORITY—AUTHORITY FIGURE, ELECTED OFFICIAL,
THE BOSS, WIZARD, EXPERT, AUTHOR, CONSULTANT,
CELEBRITY

S SOUND—MICROPHONES, MUSIC, EVENT NOISE

T THIRST—ALCOHOL, BREAKS IN MEETINGS, COULD
THIS INCLUDE OTHER LIQUIDS? LIKE OCEAN, LAKE,
SWIMMING POOL, RAIN?

I ILLUMINATE—ROOM LIGHTING, COMPUTERS,
MOVIES, LAS VEGAS LIGHTS, SPOTLIGHT, MULTI-
MEDIA, LIGHTING OUT OF THE ORDINARY,
I.E. THE SUN

C CALORIES—MEALS, THEME-TYPE FOOD—MEXICAN,
CHINESE, CHOCOLATE, DESSERTS

"My friend, you need to share these with your team members as you educate them on **DRASTIC** and as you feel comfortable with the concepts," said Brock, slightly turning his head to the side and looking at me from the corner of his eyes. "You will find how empowering these concepts are to your team as they do their work. The creativity **DRASTIC** evokes is uplifting." Rising from his chair, he moved around to the opposite side of the table and picked up a dry eraser and was wiping away some of the leftover notes from my meeting. "Besides," he continued, "you really need to be moving your 'brands' into the realm of the 4 E's."

Chapter Seven

Six months later . . .

Things changed. I gave my team the full
load. It took one whole meeting to tell
my fellow workers about the airport, the
wedding, the *Es of Branding*. By the
next meeting, one of them had photo-
copied the sheet with possible uses for
the DRASTIC elements. We talked
about how it would apply to the things
we were working on. At first, there was
a hesitancy to try using the **DRASTIC**
elements in our work. Over the next few
weeks, as we started seeing some significant successes and positive feedback, our
confidence grew. We found that the
things we were working on seemed to
stand out a little more, and people were
having more fun. Like a large flywheel,
the momentum started slowly, but as the

various team members came to see the value of using **DRASTIC** in their efforts, the results started to grow.

The sharing of stories associated with **DRASTIC** seemed to start each of our meetings.

"Come on, Ed, tell us how it went," said one of my managers to his peer sitting across the table.

At first Ed seemed a little embarrassed to share his experience.

"Well, first I figured that since our new offering was going to be a hit, I ought to get buy-in from the distributors, so I put together a kickoff meeting here in town," said Ed.

I leaned forward to hear his report. He had gotten quite a few people involved and there was momentum within various departments.

"I figured if I got them to dedicate a couple of days of their time, that would be the equivalent of their having some skin in the game," Ed said as he leaned forward putting his elbows on the table. "Correlating with the **D** in **DRASTIC**, they would be investing in the new product with their time. And time is money, so they say. So I had my price of admission done, with time and some of their travel expenses as the dollars associated with **D**." He bent over and picked up a box and set it on the conference table, unfolded the lid, and started tossing each of us a bright red golf shirt. There on the front was the logo for his new offering. "Here you go, folks. The **R** for the *raiment* of **DRASTIC**."

"So, Ed, what about your authority figure?" I asked.

Ed grinned. "That was easy," he said. "I asked the lead engineer of development to come and take the group on a tour of the manufacturing facility. As they experienced the sound, lights, and noise of production and heard the excitement of our expert, their enthusiasm grew. I guess I ticked off the **A** for *Authority* and the **S** for the ***sounds*** of the plant at the same time. After the tour, and the subsequent rollout meetings, I took the group of distributors out for drinks and dinner at that new 'eatertainment' spot down the street—you know the one with the themed jungle décor. I figure that allowed me to cover the **T**, **I**, and **C** parts of **DRASTIC** for the ***Thirst***, the ***Illumination*** and the ***Calories***. I would recommend the chocolate pie dessert to you," he said as he patted his belly to chuckles from the team members.

"I think it went well, because the evaluations and feedback were great," he said as he dropped a stack of papers on the table.

Chapter Eight

Time goes by . . .

I started to see **DRASTIC** in my day-to-day world. Parts of it were sprinkled in places where I found myself as the satisfied customer—places where I returned again and again. Some of them even surprised me at first. I found myself ticking off the elements as I sat and waited for my car to be worked on at the repair shop.

After picking up the car I went in to get my wife from the salon where she was getting her hair done. This place had all of the **DRASTIC** elements. While the customers waited, the salon had finger foods and a coffee latte machine. The receptionist was wearing an impeccable, starched smock and was asking me if I needed assistance. As I sat and waited, she orchestrated the comings and goings of freshly coiffed women, with the sound of classical jazz in the background.

Then there was the training event in the office. As we entered the room, the lights were dimmed and upbeat music thumped out of a table top sound system. The training tables were covered with paper which was topped with squishy balls, building blocks, assorted "executive" toys, colored pencils, and markers. An action video was projected onto the wall, but if it had any sound you couldn't hear it with the music that was filling the room. The setting vibrated with activity and excitement. People had cups of coffee or juice and gathered in various groups talking over the sound of the music. Others were gathered at a continental breakfast in the back of the room. The trainer, dressed in a NFL football jersey with matching baseball hat, approached me and asked for my "ticket." As I pulled the piece of paper out of my shirt pocket, I realized she had filled the **D** in the **DRASTIC** requirement with a fake dollar-looking "ticket" for admittance. I momentarily recalled the curiosity that ticket caused when I got it a few weeks earlier, making a mental note that this was a little different than anything I had seen from the training department. It was attached to a piece of paper that indicated dress for the event REQUIRED a shirt, hat, or piece of clothing that reflected each individual's favorite sports team.

As I stood there waiting for the training to start, I mentally checked off the **DRASTIC** elements. I thought that if there ever was a place where drastic change was needed it was in organization development.

In most cases, people were using parts of **DRASTIC**, but those events that really stuck out were those where my employees dared to push each element with a little **creativity** and **innovation**. In many cases, they were able to get huge impact without spending a lot of money.

❝those events that really stuck out were those where my employees dared to push each element with a little creativity and innovation...❞

One of my favorite observations was someone who orchestrated inexpensive materials for a very memorable event. It was a product launch . . . the Chocolate Party.

We had hired a new marketing manager from outside the company and brought her on board to help us launch a new business unit. She announced a kick-off meeting and sent an e-mail invite to everyone in the building.

I arrived a half hour late from the official start time to find people coming out of the large conference room with smiles on their faces. The music bumping from the room hit me in the face as I rounded the corner.

As I stepped into the room, I remember thinking, "Toto, we are not in Kansas anymore."

The lights were turned off. Tables had been clustered together in the center of the room, and they had been set with various layers, terraces and plateaus— each with a different dish sat in the midst of bunched-up white table-cloths. Strung all around the dishes were strands of white Christmas tree lights. Since most of the dishes were crystal, the combination of lights and glass, each set at a different height, made for a sparkling presentation in the dim room.

In the various dishes were all things chocolate. Chocolate cakes, Boston Crème pies, M&Ms, hand dipped chocolates, chocolate bars standing on their ends and poking out of an oversized wine glass. A chef in white starched hat and smock stood at the back of this "island" of chocolate dishes slicing pieces of several rich looking desserts and putting them on plates for attendees. People with their plates full of decadence and calories made their way over to the side of the room where spotlights highlighted the new product line. There, the product manager and her team stood and shook hands, answered questions and passed out samples to anyone who was interested.

The buzz her event created was immeasurable. It really could be seen as a classic example of the branding E's of Equity and the triangle of Experiences, Expectations and Events. Her kickoff event sent a message of something new, different, and exciting. It definitely qualified as **DRASTIC**.

Chapter Nine

In the future . . .

The conversations on **DRASTIC** change seemed long ago. I looked up as Brock came out of the darkness and walked to my side. He extended his hand for a quiet handshake as the sound of laughter and applause erupted from the hidden audience. We both gazed towards the bright lights of the stage from our protected position next to the lighting stagehand beside his panel of controls. Brock pointed at the table that was in the middle of the stage with its remaining crystal trophies and with a grin whispered, "look. . . *DRASTIC*."

It was the end of the awards ceremony, and we were there to receive dual recognition for our efforts and success. Profits on both of our product lines had climbed and as our status grew, we were singled out in several industry magazines and stories.

The division president started reading the introduction to our grand entrance from the teleprompter as images from our programs and campaigns flashed on the large screen behind him.

I turned to Brock and whispered, "I have a couple of questions for you."

"Now?" he questioned.

"Why? Why did you tell me about **DRASTIC**? We wouldn't be sharing the stage now if I hadn't started using the principles."

Shifting his weight and leaning in close he said, "Because I am leaving the company."

My jaw dropped. "What?"

"Yes. About the time I started using

DRASTIC in my business, I shared it with a couple of my siblings. Their business took off also. Now they want me to come and work in 'the family business.' Their little enterprise is booming. As my brothers and sisters talked about me coming into the business, I thought it would be an act of friendship to share **DRASTIC** with you before I left."

Hundreds of other questions were now crowding into my mind when he brought me back with, "You said you had a couple of questions."

"Other questions? Oh, right. You know, I have wondered about the guy in the airport."

"What airport?"

"You know, the guy who was having the conversation with your father, as they were waiting for the storms to blow through."

"Oh, THAT guy," said Brock.

"I wondered if you ever found out who he was or any more information about him."

Brock had a look of total surprise. "You mean I never told you who he was? Wow. I guess that really does make DRASTIC more powerful."

"What? You mean he is somebody I would know?" I asked.

"Yes, by all means. As I have watched the results of how he applied **DRASTIC** in his business, I'm amazed more people don't use these principles."

"Great," I said. "But who is he?"

"It would be better to say, who WAS he. My father's journal indicated that his airport friend was on his way to Florida to buy ground for an extremely large business venture. He did, indeed, start on that venture which has touched the lives of untold millions, although he never saw it completed."

Just then the voice from the dais rose in crescendo with "Folks, will you help me congratulate this year's winners of our highest award of achievement..." as the applause started to grow.

Brock looked at me; put his arm across my shoulders as we started walking into the lights. He turned his head and with a wink said, "His name was ... "Walt.""

Epilog

"May I help you?" she asked as she laid down her telephone handset.

"I don't have an appointment or anything" I stammered. "I was out this way for a meeting and stopped to see an old friend. Is it possible that Brock is in and available?"

Her phone erupted with some sort of 'I want attention. . . . right now' sound, but before she picked it up she indicated that she would check and "Would you mind having a seat for a minute?"

To say that the reception area was busy would be an understatement. It seemed as if every seat and table top had someone holding conversations, reviewing documents, or making phone calls. The energy and success of my friend's company was apparent by the climate and buzz, even here in the lobby.

In a few minutes I turned to see Brock bound around a corner, all smiles in tow.

By the time we had walked the hall to his office, I had been introduced to at least 8 different people. Again I found myself across a table from my friend, this table a rich cherry finish that matched his other office furniture. The pleasantries of how I was doing and a 15 minute update on the latest in office politics and activities at our old company were pleasant.

He leaned back, locked his hands behind his head and wryly said, "You are not going to believe this. I have another book you ought to see." Twisting in his chair, he daftly scooped up a spiral bound book off the corner of his desk.

"Remember that I said my siblings wanted me to come to work in this business?"

"Yeah, so?"

"Remember my younger brother, the football player?"

"The one that played until his knees got so banged up?"

"That's the one." Brock dropped the book with a slap onto the table and peeled open the front cover. "After his injuries, my brother went to work for a former coach." He spun the book on the table for me to see the inside cover. There was the familiar picture of a recognized celebrity coach.

"After he left coaching he disappeared while creating a little company. While his startup was struggling, he wisely hired a seasoned old salesman to help lagging revenues."

"The two of them developed a fantastic relationship and mutual understanding of each other's expertise. As they brought in extra resources, like my brother, to help make their dreams explode, they developed this." He closed the cover and slid the book toward me.

I fingered the cover and shrugged, "So what?"

"You are wondering why with so many books on success, sales, and business strategies, why this one has me interested" Brock asked. "We have been using this one to fuel our triple digit growth every year since I left the old company."

"This great coach," he went on, "has put together a simple and elegant method to gather an individual's or company's abilities and uniqueness and translate those into a sales plan that you would only get by paying a sales coach or consultant some very serious dollars.

The distinctive cover read:

The Sales Playbook

For sales skills

and

Developing your brand and marketing game plan

I looked up to see Brock grinning.

"Before you do anything "**DRASTIC**," he said with a rolling chuckle escaping his smile, "you might want to consider having a plan to win the game. Your own Playbook."

"Oh, no," I thought . . . "not again!"

About Kordell Norton

Kordell Norton is a
professional speak-
er. Besides giving
keynote addresses,
he is also a consult-
ant and graphic
facilitator for:

- Strategic & Marketing Planning

- Branding

- Sales Training

- Customer Service Training

By combining his energy, humor, and a
rich business background in sales and
management, he creates wonderful training events for his customers.

In addition to his years as a speaker,
consultant, trainer and facilitator, he has
held executive positions in multi-billion

dollar corporations as a vice president over 500 agents in several Call Centers as well as a Director of Human Resources. He has had responsibilty for a $31 million dollar marketing budget to drive $2.5 billion in sales, and many years in sales and sales management.

As a member of the National Speakers Association he fuses his ability to speak and entertain with skills as a certified graphic facilitator. He uses large scale, wall-sized graphics to pull the collective wisdom of groups together.

Kordell Norton loves people. His ability to get people to talk and share their insights are what his customer's indicate they value. Then there are the results that come. Those speak for themselves.

He currently lives in Twinsburg, Ohio, where he and his wife of 30 plus years enjoy their 6 great kids and the arriving grandchildren.

To have Kordell speak at your next event or to work with your team, he can be reached at www.KordellNorton.com or (330) 405-1950.

You will be glad you called.

Final Thoughts

1. Share Throwing Gas On The Fire with your business, friends and family.Buy 50 copies and get 50% discount off the retail price. Call (877) 660-4237 (toll free) for special pricing on larger quantities.

2. Share your successes. Send us your thoughts, insights, wins, and success stories. We would love to hear how these things helped so we can use those with future projects and in new projects. Mail or email to:

Hot Success
c/o Synergy Solutions
3262 Darien Lane
Twinsburg, Ohio 44087
Kordell@KordellNorton.com

3. Visit us at **www.KordellNorton.com** for additional insights, hot new information on how others have applied these ideas,

4. Thank you to my friends, family, the mastermind group, the book creation team and my second family at the National Speakers Association. These are they who encourage and support, who care and believe and build the foundation behind the faith of action. You are the treasure of this world.

QUICK ORDER FORM

Fax orders: 330-405-9828. Send this form.

Telephone orders: call 877-660-4237 toll-free.

Email orders: **renee@kordellnorton.com**

Postal Orders: eScholars, 3262 Darien Lane, Twinsburg, Ohio 44087, USA

Telephone: 330-405-1950

Please send the following books, disk or reports. I understand that I may return any of them for a full refund – for any reason, no questions asked.

_____

_____

_____

Please send more FREE information on:

- ◦ Other Books
- ◦ Speaking/Seminars
- ◦ Consulting

Name:_____

Address:_____

City:_____

State:_____ Zip: _____

Email: _____

Sales Tax: Products shipped to Ohio may be subject to additional sales tax

Note: Shipping rates will vary based on quantities, method of shipment, etc.

QUICK ORDER FORM

Fax orders: 330-405-9828. Send this form.

Telephone orders: call 877-660-4237 toll-free.

Email orders: **renee@kordellnorton.com**

Postal Orders: eScholars, 3262 Darien Lane, Twinsburg, Ohio 44087, USA

Telephone: 330-405-1950

Please send the following books, disk or reports. I understand that I may return any of them for a full refund – for any reason, no questions asked.

_____

_____

_____

Please send more FREE information on:

- Other Books

- Speaking/Seminars

- Consulting

Name:_____

Address:_____

City:_____

State:_____ Zip: _____

Email: _____

Sales Tax: Products shipped to Ohio may be subject to additional sales tax

Note: Shipping rates will vary based on quantities, method of shipment, etc.